Donna Spencer

PRESENTING
DESIGN WORK

Publisher: Donna Spencer

https://maadmob.com.au

TABLE OF CONTENTS

FOREWORD

If you work in the tech industry and have anything to do with design, chances are you've had to present your work to clients or team members at some point. The process can be excruciating: gathering all of the information you think you need to include, practicing (or not) what you plan to say, losing sleep the night before. When presentation day comes, you find yourself in front of a roomful of people—some expectant, some distracted, some disinterested, and some who ask "questions" afterward that invariably seem to derail the conversation.

Presentations have a way of triggering self-doubt. Yes, we want to share our work and help others understand it better, and it's wonderful to have our skills as designers confirmed. But if we feel like our work isn't understood or valued, we can start to wonder whether or not we're cut out for it. If only we were free to do the creative problem-solving we're so good at without having to present it to a tough crowd!

As a professional keynote speaker, author, and former web designer slash front-end developer, I'm intimately familiar with the relationship between creativity, presenting, and self-doubt. And I'm pleased to report that although preparing and giving presentations will probably always seem like a daunting amount of work, Donna Spencer has written a book that will make the process more straightforward and less excruciating.

I first met Donna in 2015 when I keynoted GIANT Conference. She immediately impressed me with her extensive experience, keen smarts, deep knowledge of the UX industry, and fantastic sense of humor. In 2016, I got to know Donna even better when she invited me to keynote UX Australia. It was then that I saw firsthand her deep commitment to strengthening the UX community through creating an event filled with relevant, meaningful content.

This book is a condensed version of much of what I've experienced of Donna as a person—but with a laser-like focus on presenting design work. She has taken her years of experience, love of teaching, and drive to help people work better and has woven them, with great wit and care, into a series of easy-to-follow steps.

There's a common misconception that presenting well stems from natural ability—that polished speakers don't ever doubt themselves or get nervous, and that effective presenters don't need to prepare in advance. Nothing could be further from the truth. Presenting anything well comes from having the right mental approach, knowing the proper steps and structure required to present effectively to an audience, and putting in lots (and lots) of practice.

That's where Donna's book comes in. By pragmatically laying out the steps required to nail any and every design presentation you give, it aims to help you fine-tune your mind-set in a way that will completely transform how you think about and approach presenting design work. This book will benefit not only design professionals who struggle to present their work, but anyone who needs to present creative problem-solving to colleagues and stakeholders.

—Denise Jacobs

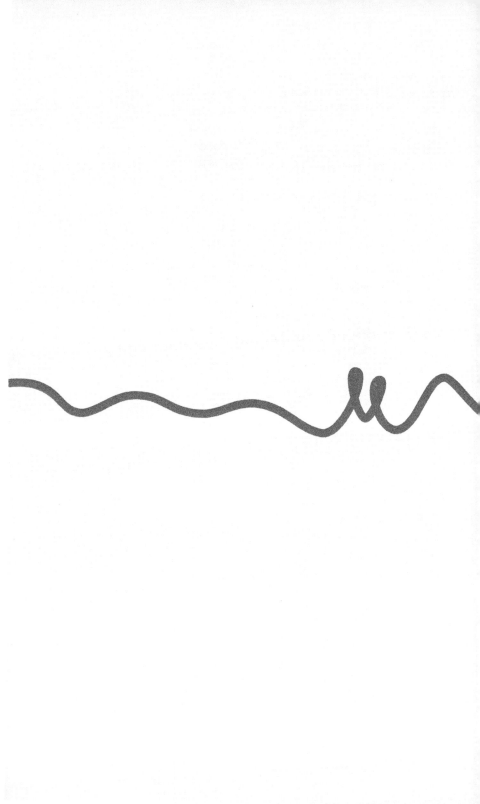

ONE OF THE MOST important skills for designers to have is to be able to effectively present design work and get feedback on it. It's very likely it's the activity we do most often after design itself.

And yet, we aren't usually taught how to do it. It isn't part of most design school curricula (and not all designers went to school anyway). Design books and blogs cover presentation briefly, at best. I, like many others I've talked to, just figured it out as I went along.

Luckily, I'm a natural presenter and storyteller. Standing in front of an audience—small or large—has never been a problem for me. Confidence and improvisation aren't a problem (people who know me will be nodding fiercely at this). So I didn't really think about how difficult presentations were until I started leading and coaching designers. Only then did I realize that, for most people, presenting work is very stressful and very scary.

I think this has two sources. The first comes from the general difficulty of presenting; the second involves a real lack of clarity about *why* we present in the first place.

On the surface, it seems that we present our work to show what we've done—to demonstrate progress, communicate our skills, and present the actual designs. What's less obvious is that presenting isn't actually about presenting. It's more about listening, communicating, and inviting other people into the design process. Showing something off is just a way to get more involvement.

That's why this book focuses on the other people in the room as much as the presenter themselves. While I do, of course, talk about how to present your design work effectively, just as much of the book covers how to get the best out of your audience.

The 'design work' I talk about in this book is mostly the sort of work a user will eventually interact with. Think screens, devices, and services. Much of the advice in these pages is relevant to presenting visual branding and research as well, and I've included some suggestions for this in the Resources section.

This little book covers the following:
- The story of a presentation that didn't go well
- Why we present design work
- How to consider the audience and plan to work with them
- How to present the work
- How to prepare, rehearse, and manage the presentation
- How to get great feedback and use it

It's intended as a short, practical book that you can read quickly and improve your presentations immediately. If you've felt stressed and frustrated by how your presentations have gone in the past, I hope the advice you find here will help you improve the very next one you give.

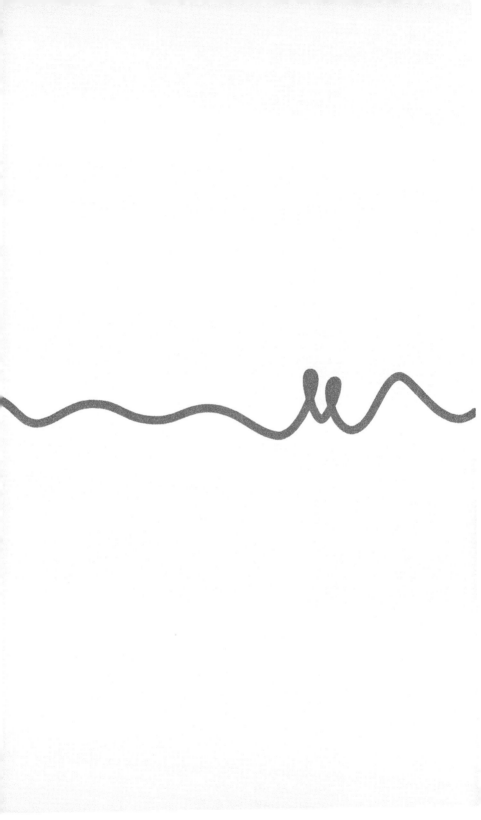

It's Tuesday afternoon: time for the team to present its progress to the client and stakeholders. They've been working on a website for local businesses to promote used and repaired items. Alex, the lead designer, has not been looking forward to this afternoon—it's the third presentation, and she just doesn't seem to be getting through to the clients.

Alex has been worrying about this all day. She finished the slides half an hour ago and got to the meeting room a few minutes early. But now she can't figure out how to show both the slides and the prototype screens; when one is working, the other one won't display properly. Her colleague Josh leans over her shoulder and points to the button that switches it over. Phew! Just in time.

She sees someone she hasn't seen in previous meetings— nicely dressed, with a neat purple blazer—maybe an account manager? She also notices fewer people than last week but can't tell who's missing.

She gets going. "Hi guys—oops, I mean… everyone… thanks for coming. We've done a lot since the last presentation. I'll show you where we got to." She opens up the first screen of the prototype. "Oh, that's not the right screen." Slightly frazzled, she quickly zooms out to find the right one and starts again. Priya, a product manager who has attended all of the meetings so far, begins to feel a little seasick from the rapid on-screen scrolling.

The first version of the homepage features a big search box in the middle, which is what the marketing manager, Grant, advised against in the last meeting; it might be okay for users, but it's not great for the businesses the client is trying to promote. Before Grant can raise his hand to ask about this, though, Alex explains that they've ruled this one out already, and quickly shifts to a second version, with a carousel of product photos. This one, Alex explains, would be great for the businesses, but would not make it easy for users to find what they wanted. Already feeling that the meeting is a waste of time, Grant begins writing notes to prep for his customer calls this afternoon and has mostly tuned out by the time Alex shows the third version, which the team decided was a good mix of the first two.

Alex points out everything visible on the page: the navigation, the dropdown menu at the side of the page, the map that filters location, the carousel of product photos, and the keyword search. Mei, the developer, begins to worry she won't have anything to contribute to this meeting, just like the last one. As Alex changes the screen, Mei seizes the opportunity and interjects, "Carousels don't scale well to mobile—is there a different plan for how mobile displays might work?"

Grant looks up and is struck by the tangerine color used on the page; it reminds him of one of their competitor's apps. "I don't mean to interrupt," he interrupts, "but is this the final color scheme?"

"Hold on, please—I'll take questions at the end." Alex forges ahead. She's lost her train of thought now and stumbles over a few words before remembering what she meant to say. Right, the storefront page. She points out the business logo and business description, and then describes how the products will be displayed on the page. She notices a few people writing notes and shuffling, looking like they're getting ready to talk, so she speeds up to head off any more interruptions.

She quickly moves on to the third screen, which contains details about a product that can be purchased. She points out the large product photo and explains that users will be able to hover over it to get a quick view. She points out the dropdowns to select size and color. She explains that, for users who are logged in, the related products will be personalized based on what they have previously purchased.

Finally, she's on the last slide. She got through it! She turns to the group and asks, "What do you think?"

The comments and questions fly back at her:

- "My sister would really love this. How would she add her store to the service?"
- "Are you going to use that font?"
- "Can we make sure people can't narrow down the location too much? We want to make sure as many businesses as possible come up in the results."
- "Are you using AI to improve the recommendations?"
- "Does it work on an iPhone?"
- "Can you make the buttons rounder? They look too square."

Alex scrambles to make some notes. She hadn't anticipated these kinds of questions, most of which don't even seem to be related to what she just showed.

"We've already finished the designs for business sign-up. I showed them during the last meeting." Really, when will Priya let this one go? She's asked some version of this question at every meeting so far. "No, we're not going to use that font. At the moment, we're wireframing the core features; we'll work on the visual approach once the wireframes are signed off." Why are they always asking about the font? It's not important at this point. "We haven't detailed how the location filter will work yet. Yes, the site will work on an iPhone." She ignores the question about AI – that's technical and she doesn't know the answer.

Alex walked out of that presentation feeling frustrated. She's sure the work is good, but the stakeholders didn't react well. Every week, they ask the same questions and give feedback that isn't relevant. She knows she prepared, but she completely forgot to go through the slides she made—it gets so hectic trying to keep ahead of people's questions and comments.

The clients walked out of the presentation feeling frustrated as well. The presentation was too fast for them to understand; it was hard to figure out which screens were the final ones, and they didn't know what they were being asked to look at. They felt like their questions hadn't been answered and still didn't know how to get them answered.

WHEN PRESENTATIONS GO RIGHT

Presentations can be much better than this. Here's what happens in a great presentation:
- The audience understands what's happening and what's expected of them.
- Stakeholders listen, ask smart, relevant questions, and give feedback that's related to their expertise (instead of opinion).
- You feel calm, confident, and in control.
- The entire team walks away able to create a much better product.

But how do we get there? Let's start with understanding why we present our work in the first place.

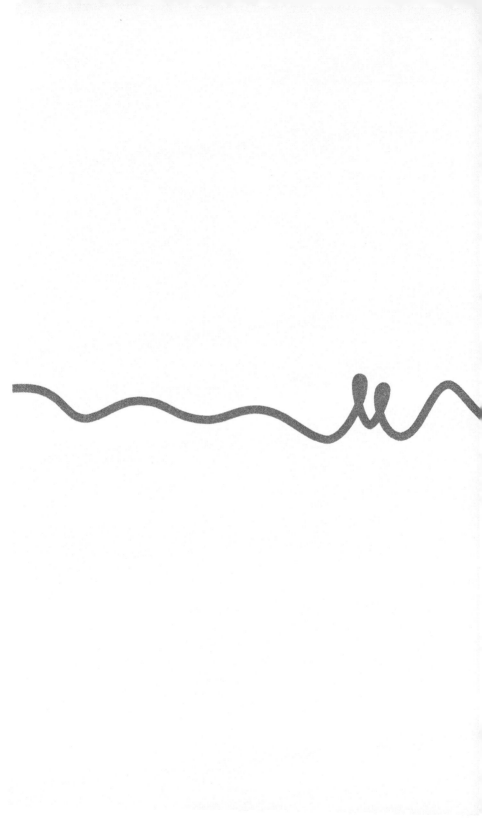

As DESIGNERS, WE PRESENT a lot. We are constantly showing our work—sometimes to a fellow team member, sometimes to a client. Sometimes it's a casual chat; other times, it's more formal, and the entire success of the project hinges on it.

Why do we do present so much? Why do I suggest it's a core skill for designers?

Ultimately, the reason we share our work is to get broader input and set ourselves up to make the best possible product or service.

PRESENTING ISN'T ABOUT YOU

Creating a product or service is not a solo undertaking. It belongs to a team—often quite a large one.

- There is usually someone in a business who owns the overall product. This person also usually owns the *risk*. They're responsible for what happens when the product or service goes out into the world. Although designers sometimes think they make the design decisions, ultimately, it's this person who makes final decisions about the design—it's their risk they're managing.
- There are usually subject-matter experts. These people know about legislation and regulations, understand how work actually happens, and grasp the nitty-gritty details of the real world. They will usually have a good understanding of unusual situations or requirements. They often know what the edge cases are and what might go wrong.
- Front-line staff members know about all the situations users find themselves in. They understand the wide variety of uses a product or service will be put to. They may also be the ones who will ultimately have to deal with any poor design decisions.

- Developers build digital products. They have a solid understanding of what is easy to implement and what is hard. They might have built something similar, and know what will trip the design up. They know how database efficiency, security, and performance will affect the product. They can offer alternative approaches to achieve the design outcome.

All of these people play a significant role in the design. They have important and valuable input. They also probably have other things to do, so their only chance to contribute is at presentation time.

Apart from actually creating the design, the main job of a designer is to help other people make good and informed decisions. Designers themselves don't usually get to make final decisions about the product or service—they advise. And they do this via a lot of discussions, a lot of presentations, and a lot of listening.

When I meet designers who express concerns about their presentations, often it's because they feel that presenting is a validation of their value and their skills, which makes it hard not to take criticism very personally.

The best thing I can do for these designers is help remove ego from the equation. Presenting your work is not about getting a pat on the back, validation of your skills, or congratulations for doing well. It's about using the skills and experience of a larger, more diverse group of people to improve the product or service.

When designers don't think they need to share their work, don't want to ask for feedback, and don't want to make changes as a result of feedback, it shows that there is a problem in the design process. Sometimes designers have a lack of confidence; sometimes, they feel a lot of ownership over the design; sometimes, it's just how they saw designers work in a previous job. What's common is that these designers haven't realized that the whole team owns the design.

TYPES OF PRESENTATIONS

Design presentations are about discussions and decisions. Some presentations lean more toward the discussion end of the spectrum, others more toward the decision end. Each type has a different level of formality and a different kind of feedback process.

Presenting regular progress

The least formal and most frequent type of presentation is the regular check-in with a project team to discuss progress. If you're working as part of a team on a long-running project, you'll be doing these a lot.

In this kind of presentation, your goal will be to show progress and get ongoing feedback and input from the team. You'll be showing the design itself, asking questions of the team, checking assumptions, and discussing feasibility. You'll definitely be listening more than you'll be presenting.

A regular team should know how the project is tracking and who is responsible for what. You should be able to collect feedback, discuss options, and make decisions on the spot.

Presenting the current state

A slightly more formal type of presentation is a regularly scheduled meeting that may be open to a broad group of people, mainly to show the current state of a project. Many Agile teams call this something like *showcase*. If you're working in a consulting capacity (where the project team works together, often offsite), your regular project check-ins will usually have this level of formality.

The goals of this kind of presentation are to show the current state of the design and to collect quality feedback.

Note that I didn't say "show you've made progress" here. In my experience, these sorts of presentations have a revolving group of people who pop in when they can. They don't attend regularly enough to care about progress; they care about the current state. Because people attend infrequently, they may want to give feedback on parts of the design that are already resolved, as we saw with Priya's question to Alex about the business sign-up page in the example presentation. (We'll learn more about how to manage infrequent participants in Chapter 3.)

In this kind of presentation, you'll focus mainly on the problems the design solves and not as much on the nitty-gritty details of each screen. When thinking about what you're going to present, make sure it clearly demonstrates how it will meet the needs of the business and shows your understanding of the broader goals.

In these presentations, you'll often have limited time, so you'll want to establish a formal feedback mechanism. You might be able to resolve some feedback in the meeting itself, but most will be followed up outside the meeting .

Presenting the final version

When consulting, and sometimes when you're working in-house, there are two contexts in which you'll present a 'final' version of a project in a quite formal way: milestones and final presentations.

The goal of these presentations is quite different from those I mentioned above. Here, the goal is to get sign-off. For some milestones, and certainly for a final presentation, the goal is to get paid.

These presentations should be well prepared and well rehearsed.

You should never give the first presentation at the same time as you are asking for sign-off. You should also not be presenting anything new at this point. If you present work in progress here, you will be frustrated that you are asked to make changes, and the client will be frustrated that you didn't get it right.

Make it clear upfront that any feedback at this point will inform the next phase of work (if there is one). Be very clear that you are asking for sign-off (and payment). Don't beat around the bush or avoid the discussion—this is what you are here to do.

Then present a summary of everything you have presented before. Don't add anything new. There should be nothing new to react to and no surprises for the client.

If the client attempts to give feedback, change their mind, or ask for additional work (and they will, no matter how well you've presented in the past and how well you've managed feedback), refer back to previous discussions and decisions. Which, of course, you have been documenting and sharing all along.

If something unexpected happens, like a more senior person turning up for the first time and wanting to provide input, reiterate what you have presented in the past, the feedback you've received, and the decisions made as a group. Involve the rest of the group to support these decisions. And during the next round, make sure that senior person is involved throughout.

PRESENT EARLY AND OFTEN

A key thing to remember about presentations is that there should be plenty of them.

Some teams make the mistake of having only a few presentations, with the first when work has been underway for some time. Don't do this—people will feel like they aren't being allowed to contribute, and their feedback can undo a lot of work.

The most common reason for delaying a presentation is "we don't have enough to show". The common excuses for few presentations are "they take too long" and "every time we show them something they change their mind". If you set up a presentation and feedback process early on and teach the client how to give good feedback, you'll avoid these problems. Your client will get comfortable with you showing them small amounts of work more frequently, the presentations will be fast, and you won't have to manage dramatic changes in direction. The changes that do occur will tend to come earlier and will be easier to handle.

It's also not uncommon for clients to see the first presentation and realize that you are on the wrong track—perhaps because they didn't know what they really needed. You want to catch this as early as you possibly can.

ALEX RETHINKS HER PRESENTATION GOALS

Let's return for a moment to Alex's story from Chapter 1. It sounds like Alex had been presenting often and was interested in asking for feedback. That's a great start!

Her Tuesday meeting was the second type—a fairly formal presentation about current state that people might attend when they can. Although we didn't have insight into what Alex was thinking as she prepared, it didn't appear that she'd thought about the goal of the presentation, the style, and what type of things to talk about. As a result, her presentation was very similar to a progress update—a bit too informal for the audience she ended up facing.

Because this was a formal meeting with unexpected participants, Alex should have focused more on the business problems than on individual screens, considered who was there and why, and planned for feedback.

The good news is that Alex's next meeting goes much more smoothly. She thought about the presentation goals, which were to get feedback on the overall approach for the current feature. She shows far fewer screens as a result, and the commentary is much more focused.

Now, let's take a closer look at how to run both the room and the presentation more effectively.

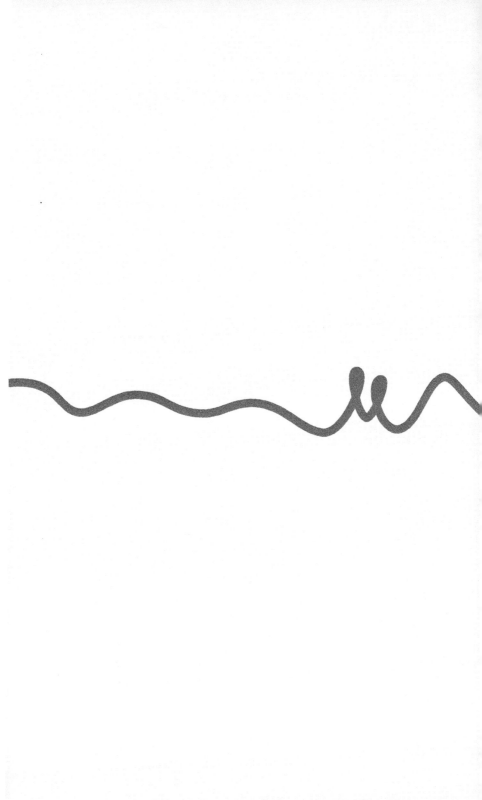

You may think that planning your design presentation should be all about figuring out how to show your great design. Yes, that's important—and we'll discuss it more in Chapter 4. But the truly hard part—the part we'd all like to ignore—is planning for the crowd.

Every presentation has an audience, and you have more control over how they react and behave than you think, as long as you're deliberate about it.

PLAN FOR YOUR AUDIENCE

As I mentioned in Chapter 2, different types of meetings have different types of participants. For regular team meetings, you'll usually know everyone. For more formal meetings, there might be people who you've never met before, and there might be people missing.

People you already know

When planning your presentation, first think about the people you already know and have had meetings with before. Think about what their role is, what their skills are, and what they are interested in (these things may not be the same). Consider the questions they ask every time and the topics they seem to care most about. For example, Alex should have been able to predict that Mei would ask about performance on mobile and could have explained it before Mei even posed the question.

People you don't know

Because presenting is about listening, you need to know who you are listening to. You need to know who is watching your presentation and why. If you don't know this, you cannot possibly use their input to achieve the presentation's goals.

Do everything you can ahead of time to find out who will be in the presentation. Find out who has been invited, who has said they can attend, and who has said they can't. Find out what their roles are, how often they'll be involved, and whether they influence or make decisions.

If you're working as a consultant with an external client, don't be afraid to talk to your contact to find out the answers to these questions. It is the professional, organized thing to do.

Sometimes this is difficult, and sometimes people will simply turn up unannounced. That's okay—it doesn't need to fluster you or mess up your presentation. Always leave time at the beginning of the presentation or meeting to see who is in the room and why they are there. If you find yourself in a room with people you don't know, ask for introductions. Yes, they might already know one another, but you can't present effectively if you don't know who is there and what matters to them.

People new to the project

If you know someone new to the project will be attending a presentation, arrange to meet with them beforehand, and show them everything you've covered in previous presentations. That way, they won't disrupt the presentation by asking questions or giving feedback on features that have been finalized.

People who aren't there

There are many reasons why people can't attend a presentation. If you know someone can't make it (and they are a key subject-matter expert or decision-maker), arrange to catch up with them outside the presentation. Give them the opportunity to hear the same presentation as everyone else and to give their feedback in the same way.

Often, someone will come to the presentation, go back to their team to get feedback from their group. This can make feedback more difficult. They will never be able to present like you can—they won't understand the details to the same extent, and they don't know where to focus. They probably won't be able to answer questions from their team. Usually, the feedback that trickles back in this manner is neither useful nor usable.

Consider whether you can present to these people directly. That might mean you need to present more often to smaller groups, but it will also mean you get much better feedback and input. If I simply cannot present to people (which I find often happens in healthcare and customer support), I record a short video or give them a set of scenarios and a clickable prototype. It's not the same as talking directly, but it's better than secondhand feedback.

People who are disruptive

Admittedly, it's not easy to plan for disruptive participants. The two types I see most often are people who have a position to push and people who want to revisit decisions that have already been finalized.

If you know who will be there and understand what matters to them, you're already somewhat prepared. If you've arranged to talk to new people or people who missed a presentation, that goes a long way as well. Giving everyone a clear role in the presentation (which I'll discuss in the next section) will also help a lot.

People tend to revisit decisions either when they are made too quickly, without enough reflection and discussion, or when they feel like they haven't been heard. They will derail your presentations until their feedback is considered. If this happens to you a lot, look at how you are collecting feedback, and ask yourself whether you are giving people enough time to reflect and contribute. (We'll cover feedback in more detail in chapter 6.)

PREPARE THE AUDIENCE

Once you have a sense of who will be in the presentation and why, you can be very deliberate about how you involve them in the presentation.

Give people a job

One of the biggest mistakes designers make when they present is giving participants free rein to give feedback and ask questions about whatever they like—whether or not they know anything about the topic.

When you show a design and ask for feedback, people will give feedback. Their feedback may or may not be related to any expertise they have, may be an opinion, or may be a random thought. Very few people have the confidence to say, "I don't think I can offer anything here" or "Looks good to me." Almost everyone will feel they need to contribute. And the more senior they are, the more they will feel they need to.

This is why a lot of feedback is not useful or usable. It's why people will comment on the color or the font or suggest that the corners on the button should be rounder. They just feel the need to say *something*.

Prepare for this by giving people clear instructions on what their role in the presentation is and what you do and don't want to know about. When you give people a job to do, they'll focus on that.

If your audience is made up of representatives from different roles (e.g., project sponsors, managers, developers, other designers), you might be able to give them jobs that relate to their specific role and expertise. Try to avoid stereotyping and pigeonholing them, though—think about what their skills and interests are as well, since most people have expertise outside of their role description.

If your audience is made up of a particular kind of role (e.g., all front-line staff), give them all the same jobs to do, but still be specific about what they should focus on.

And of course, if you have a mix, adapt the approach to your actual audience.

The key thing is to give everyone something specific to think about and to emphasize that you want their expertise.

Examples of what you might ask people to focus on include questions like these:

- Will this design work for the core user group and core tasks?
- Will the design work for the content?
- Is there terminology that users won't understand?
- Are there user tasks / edge cases the design won't work for?
- Is there anything technically difficult we haven't considered?
- Is there overlap with work being done by another team?
- Does the design adhere to brand guidelines or the style guide? (When you are specific about who can focus on the visual aspects, the rest of the room will pay less attention to it)

This doesn't need to take long. You can do it verbally or make it a slide in a presentation. Decide how formal you want to be based on how long you've worked with this group.

The most important time to get this right is during your first presentation to a group or the first time a new stakeholder is involved. This is the crucial moment to teach people that they have a specific role and that you want them to contribute their expertise, not their opinions.

Explain the feedback process

Before you start on the presentation itself, take a moment to explain how the feedback process will work. This helps people understand how to participate in the presentation and what they should do. It also lets them know that you are listening and that you value their contribution.

If this presentation is the first in a project or the first for a group, or if you are introducing a new feedback process, take extra time with this. Most people haven't been involved in such a deliberate, structured feedback process before, and it's such an important part of the presentation experience as a whole that it's worth emphasizing.

Explain the presentation process

Let people know how the presentation will be structured—ideally, that you'll run through the whole thing and then discuss it at the end.

People usually only interrupt because they're worried they won't get an opportunity to contribute. I've noticed that if they know there's time for questions at the end, they pay more attention to the presentation, instead of trying to figure out how to get their idea heard.

Set the context

Let people know what is in and out of scope—what you'll be discussing, what you won't be discussing, and why. When context and scope aren't clear, people don't know where they are meant to focus. They go back over things that have already been discussed or jump ahead to things that aren't yet relevant.

First, explain where you are in the project—what has happened before and what will happen later. Are you 30% done or 90% done? Then explain what you will cover in this presentation—the features, screens, or user tasks. Then tell them what you will not cover.

If it is relevant, remind the group of what you've collectively decided before. Be very clear about this so they know not to go there again.

Then, reiterate the scope of the presentation and what you'll be covering. Yes, I deliberately said that twice.

ALEX INTRODUCES HERSELF AT LAST

We didn't see the steps Alex followed to prepare for the Tuesday meeting, but it sounds like she didn't think at all about who would be there. She spotted someone she'd never seen before, as well as another person whose role wasn't clear to her.

For this week's meeting, Alex checks the invite to see who is likely to attend. She notices that Grant has said no, and makes a mental note to reach out to him after the meeting. She sees that someone called Grace is planning to come, and wonders if that was the person in the purple blazer.

As it happens, the mysterious woman is in the meeting again (this time in a green blazer). Alex goes up to her with her hand outstretched for a handshake and says, "Thanks for coming! I'm not sure we've met. I'm Alex, the designer on the team." The woman smiles immediately. "Hi! I'm Grace. I'm from legal."

Alex starts the meeting by greeting everyone and thanking them for attending. "We're going to do something a bit different this week," she says. "Instead of general feedback, I'd like for you to keep an eye on specific things in the design." Because she hasn't yet learned about people's particular concerns, she decides to ask everyone to focus on the same questions, except for one technical question for Mei.

She shows a slide containing the following questions:

- Will local shoppers understand, at a glance, what the service is offering?
- Will local shoppers find the homepage interesting enough to click through to explore a product?
- Will the service give local businesses enough exposure that they will be likely to sign up?
- Is there anything that seems technically difficult? (Mei)

Alex explains that she'll run through the designs quickly and will take questions at the end. She adds that they're just going to be focusing on how people can get to the product pages today and that they'll look at that page in more detail next week.

And now that she has prepared for her audience, she can proceed to the heart of the matter: the presentation.

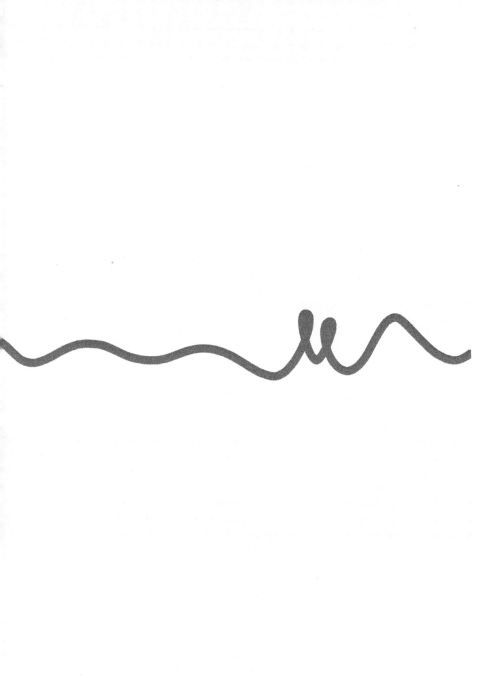

You've prepared for your audience; now you're ready to present your work. This will usually make up the bulk of the presentation, and it's your chance to make the design come to life.

EXPLAIN THE PROBLEM YOU ARE SOLVING

Before you dive into the design, describe the problem you are trying to solve. This does two things: it reinforces the scope and context for the design work and helps the audience focus on what the problem is.

Describe both sides of the problem: the business and user problem, using the same sequence your client uses. If they usually talk about the user problem they are trying to solve, start with that. If they typically talk about the business problem they are trying to solve, start with that. But make sure you cover both sides of the problem. In Alex's example, the people in the meeting always talk about how to promote local businesses that sell secondhand products, so she knows that she should first reinforce that she understands what they are trying to do.

This doesn't need to take very long, but it is important to show that you do understand the problem you're solving and that you have been designing for it.

If you're not clear what business and user problems you are trying to solve, do get clarification before you present. Ideally, you'll have this sorted out before you start designing, but we've all worked on projects that seemed unclear or where the business and user problems didn't align. If you really can't get clarification, explain the problems as best you can—your presentation might trigger the discussion that needs to happen to make things clearer. If you're worried that you won't be able to explain the issues well and it will reflect badly on you, see if you can get someone more senior to do the explaining—after all, someone must have had at least an idea of what the project was set up to do.

START WITH THE END RESULT

When you present your design, the most important thing to show is the result you came up with.

"Of course," you say. "That's obvious."

Unfortunately, it isn't obvious. The single biggest mistake I see designers make—just like Alex did—is that they explain their process, show each version of the design they attempted, and discuss every thought, tangent, and rabbit hole they've explored since the last catch-up.

The single biggest improvement is to flip that around and just show the final result.

I understand why designers present their process. They've done a lot of hard work, solved difficult design issues, tried out different approaches, failed, and thrown away ideas. It has been hard—it took ages to come up with something that they now know is good and simple and elegant. All of that is top of mind.

But the people hearing the presentation don't care. All they are hearing is: "I thought this thing, then I changed my mind, and this was hard." Like Mei, who felt impatient during Alex's first presentation, they just want you to get to the point.

If stakeholders have questions about alternate approaches or why you didn't do something in a particular way, they'll ask you. In fact, the explanation will make more sense to them when it's given as an answer to a specific question.

"But I need to show my value," designers often tell me, "and talking through my process and what I explored is how I do that." To that I say: The end result is your value. It really shouldn't matter whether the design you have created took a day or two weeks—if the solution is good, you are providing value. If you can explain why it's good in the context of the problem it is solving, you are providing value. (Yes, I know a lot of us work in environments where we count hours, not value, but that still doesn't mean you should explain every thought you've had).

So back to the obvious statement. The first thing you should show in your presentation is the result you came up with.

SHOW 'A PERSON DOING A THING'

But how do you show this brilliant result? You demonstrate it as *a person doing a thing*. From the user's point of view.

Start with the most common user scenario for the design. Work through an end-to-end story, starting with the user's goal and ending with them completing the task (or getting as far as they can with what you've designed). Describe it from the perspective of an actual person. Give them a name and a back story; don't just talk about 'the user'.

For example, Alex could bring her presentation to life by introducing Norton, the father of a three-year-old, who needs to buy new clothes for his child. Norton likes buying (and potentially selling) items secondhand. Alex can show how Norton goes to the homepage, finds stores in his local area with children's clothes, and checks what their range looks like.

Present the scenario in one go without interruption. If you stop and point things out along the way, people will start to focus on specific features instead of the overall story.

Next, present a similar task, again from the user's perspective. Start with their goal, demonstrate the workflow, and finish with them completing the task. This time around, Alex could show Norton looking for secondhand vinyl records for himself.

I suggest starting with two core tasks that are quite similar. If some steps are repeated in both scenarios, just repeat them. Show the whole experience both times. This might feel repetitive to you, but it won't feel that way to the audience. The first time will be too quick to take it in. The second time, they can look for the things they are wondering about.

When you've covered the core user tasks, show how the experience might be similar or different for people with different needs or skills. This is a great opportunity to remind people that users are not one-size-fits-all, but have different skills and use different technologies. Demonstrate how the experience sounds to a screen reader. Show what it looks like for someone with their screen zoomed all the way in. Show what it looks like in high-contrast mode. Show how it changes when people use it on different devices or screen sizes. For example, Alex could show how the service works on mobile while Norton is out and about or for someone with limited vision using a screen reader.

Only once you've been through the flow a few times, go back to the start and explain anything you need to cover in more depth. This is the time to point out features you didn't explain when you went through the user flow, explain how those features address business goals, and discuss concerns from particular stakeholders before they ask about them. This is also a good time to explain how user research or testing contributed to the design.

Why focusing on the user works

One reason demonstrating from a user's perspective works well is that it forms a narrative. People love listening to stories, and stories stick in their memory.

Another is that it puts the user at the center of the story and focuses on them. It gives you the opportunity to communicate what matters to users with a clear and engaging story. A user-focused story doesn't talk about features or screen elements, and stops the audience from focusing on those, too.

Once your audience knows you are going to present in this narrative form, they'll interrupt less and listen to the story more. Over time, they'll also ask much better questions and will start to ask questions from a user's perspective.

The thing you absolutely, positively must not do is a *real-estate tour*—that is, a screen-by-screen walk-through of a page while pointing out its features. Alex did this during her first presentation. A walk-through doesn't put the screens in the context of a person doing a thing. It draws attention to the features instead of the tasks or benefits and will get you detailed questions and feedback about the elements on the screen instead of the overall task.

What if my work isn't screens or a user flow?

Occasionally your design work will consist of something more abstract (like a sitemap) or more detailed (like copy). These two examples don't really fit the 'person doing a thing' idea. So how do you present them?

This is where you really need to have a clear idea of what your goals are and whether a presentation is the right way to achieve them. Why would you present a sitemap without any user task to support it? Same with copy—why would you present that without a user task? What are you trying to achieve by showing these off?

In my experience, these two types of design work are the most difficult to get feedback and agreement on, simply because audiences have a hard time imagining how such work will eventually be represented, and how users will interact with it. When I've seen designers ask for sign-off for this type of work without something visual to support it, they always end up frustrated when the client changes their mind after seeing the ideas represented in a more tangible form.

I suggest you never present things like this as standalone design work—only present how they affect 'a person doing a thing'. Only then will you be able to have a productive conversation about them.

DON'T USE DESIGNER JARGON

Another advantage of demonstrating a person doing a thing is that when you focus on the user task, you will naturally be less likely to talk about the design-geek detail. Jargon is so much a part of how we communicate but try to avoid it when talking with people outside your discipline. Did you even notice that Alex used jargon like dropdown, filter, carousel, hover, and personalization? If you didn't, that's probably because you use these terms without thinking.

Think about what your audience know and understand. If you use terms they don't understand or find relevant, they'll switch off, feel stupid, or contribute their uninformed opinion—none of which will give you the feedback you need.

Just use plain, simple language. Explain clearly. Help your audience understand what they don't know.

A COMPELLING STORY PUTS THE DESIGN IN PERSPECTIVE

For this week's presentation, Alex first describes the business problem the team has been solving (promoting local businesses that sell secondhand products) to show that the team understands both the business and user needs.

Then, instead of showing three different versions of the design and explaining that only the last one was what they decided on, she shows only the final one. This gets the presentation off to a much stronger start by connecting the design to the problem immediately, without irrelevant screens in between.

Instead of pointing out the features on each page, Alex talks about Norton - she first shows him looking for clothes for his three-year-old child; then looking for vinyl for himself. Next, she demonstrates what the experience would sound like if it were read out by a screen reader, reminding the audience that not everyone uses the service the same way.

With these stories, the audience gets a good, intuitive understanding of the service, and—unlike an overly detailed, blow-by-blow tour—it only takes a few minutes.

Alex then returns to the first page and talks about the various kinds of products available, and shows different ways for people to select the location. She also shares how users have reacted to the designs.

When she opens up for feedback and discussion, the audience members are in the mindset of the user and have been paying attention to what they were asked. Their questions and feedback are a lot more focused and relevant.

The presentation is what the audience sees. What they don't see is all of the work behind the scenes that makes the presentation run smoothly. A little planning goes a long way. We'll take a look at that next.

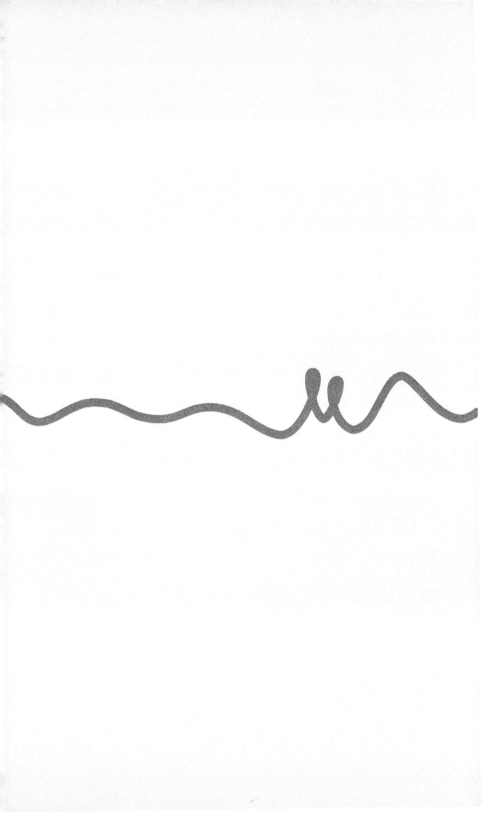

Good planning will help your presentations run smoothly and make them feel much more comfortable—not just for you but for everyone attending. Give yourself enough time for this step, particularly for assembling the presentation and rehearsing it.

PLANNING WHAT TO PRESENT

When thinking about what you'll present, consider the goals of the presentation and what feedback you need.

If you're presenting progress to your team, you might want to present with your working designs, so the team can see and respond to the changes you've made since the last check-in. If you are presenting status in a more formal setting, you'll probably have to make something specifically for that audience, so you don't accidentally show messy work in progress.

Present in the lowest fidelity that will achieve the presentation's goals. People will give feedback on what they see (even when you prepare well by giving people jobs and describing scope). If people see a beautiful, full-color, high-fidelity design with great images, that's what they'll give feedback on, and you'll lose valuable time talking about visuals when you really wanted to talk about the user flow.

If you want feedback on flow and content, show the design without imagery and color. This is a perfect time to show a rough sketch or a black-and-white wireframe. People who have never seen a wireframe before might wonder what they are looking at.

If you want feedback on layout, use some version of fake content, so people don't get caught up in the details of what the in-progress copy says. For years I've been using text from classic fiction (like *Alice in Wonderland*)—it's less confusing than lorem ipsum, and people usually smile at it and understand it.

Of course, if you want feedback on the imagery, color, transitions, and interactions, show them!

What you definitely shouldn't present is an already-built design. Not only is it harder to make changes to something that has been built, but it also communicates to your audience that you are not listening to feedback.

Planning the Presentation Format

Consider what technology will best achieve your presentation goals. You might walk through your designs in the original software you used to build them, or you might assemble a more polished slideshow presentation using a tool like PowerPoint or Keynote.

Think about whether you want control or flexibility, how you will ask people to provide feedback (which we discuss in the next chapter), and what you might need to send to people afterward.

A presentation in your favorite presentation tool:
- is good if you like to be organized and plan ahead;
- helps you stick to the flow of your planned presentation;
- is easier to rehearse;
- takes time to prepare;
- isn't as flexible: you can't show something else if someone asks a question;
- can include additional supporting materials such as research results and project progress; and
- is a good record of what was presented and easier to share with people for later review.

A wireframe or prototype demonstration:
- is good if you prefer to be flexible;
- must be set up with care and attention to detail, so you can smoothly navigate through it—if you provide the audience with a prototype link, all screens must be linked together, so people will be able to click through them

easily;

- takes time to prepare—you'll want to create a version separate from your working file;
- requires rehearsal, so you know the scenarios work well; and
- may need an additional deck or document to support it with research results or project information.

PLANNING THE NEXT PRESENTATION

Start preparing the next presentation as soon as you finish this one. Consider what you want to get out of the next presentation, then arrange the design work in between to meet those goals. This ensures you are focused on getting involvement and feedback, and your design work is directed towards that.

Also, think about the timing and feedback cycle—if it's going to take time to collect and decide on feedback, but you have another presentation due soon, you might need to work on completely different features, so you have time to address previous feedback.

SUPPORT AND NOTE-TAKING

Presenting can be a busy and intense experience. You're trying to manage equipment, tell your story, click through screens, observe the audience, and manage questions. It can be very helpful to have a second person to help out with a couple of those tasks, so you aren't juggling them all on your own.

The first job you might consider delegating is to have someone else manage the technology—not just setting it up, but also clicking through the presentation or navigating screens in the prototype as you take on the role of narrator. It's easier to tell a convincing, clear story if you can focus on the people you're talking to.

Note-taking is another area where a helper can be valuable as taking notes will interrupt the flow of your presentation. Notes are crucial for remembering what happened in the presentation and ensuring you don't later forget to address issues that came up.

You may have a colleague who can support you here (and you can return the favor during their presentations). If not, you may be able to ask someone in the audience to make notes for you. Arrange this ahead of time, so you can let them know how much detail you need and what format the notes will be in.

If you can't arrange for any note-taking support, consider recording the meeting. This may even be your default for remote presentations, where you can record and watch later to make note of the questions people asked.

If you do record the presentation, you can also use that to improve your presentation skills. Go through the recording later, note what went well and what you'd like to improve, and build them into your next presentation. Many people hate hearing or watching themselves, but it is an excellent learning tool.

REHEARSING

Practice your presentation all the way through at least once. Make sure you have your user scenarios straight, and that the presentation, wireframes, or prototype work smoothly for all of your scenarios. Think of questions that people are most likely to ask and make sure you can easily provide answers to them.

Rehearse out loud, even if it feels ridiculous. It's an important presenting trick for your brain: when you've already heard yourself say something, it's easier to do it again later on and sound more confident.

If you'll have someone helping you with the presentation, rehearse with them. This is essential if you'll be asking them to manage the technology, as it takes a couple of run-throughs to understand timing and transitions.

If you'll be in an unfamiliar room, check it out ahead of time and find out how everything works. Where are the electrical outlets? How do the light switches work? And always carry your own set of adapters—the room will never have the right one at the right time.

Remote presentations have an additional rehearsal overhead; you may need to practice screen-sharing or switching from video to a presentation. Make sure you know how to read and answer written comments. Some screen-sharing applications allow participants to "raise their hand" to ask a question; make sure you know how this works and how to manage it. You don't want to be learning the tool and presenting with it at the same time.

MANAGING THE ROOM

Before COVID, I used to do most of my presentations face to face, and preferred it. Being in a room with people allows you to connect with them and is great when the group has to work together to make decisions.

Now I present remotely almost all the time. Remote presentations can be trickier as it can be harder to interact with the group. People pay attention less, ask questions less and offer less feedback during a remote presentation, so anticipate less feedback and discussion during the presentation and perhaps more afterward.

For any kind of presentation, success largely depends on how well you manage the room—physical or virtual.

Own the room

People find it hard to ignore someone moving around at the front of a room. Our peripheral vision is wired to look up when we see movement, and our social norms have conditioned us to pay attention to the person at the front. If you stand up at the front, move, and gesture, people will look at you.

When you can, present on your feet. Own the room and take up space. Move your arms and gesture. Don't huddle behind the computer—without your physical presence, it's easy for people to get distracted.

Remotely, it's harder to do this as you need to remain in view of the camera. Make a conscious effort to sit up tall, with good posture—you'll get almost the same benefits as if you were standing up and presenting in person. Sitting up tall makes it easier to get into a pose that makes you feel confident. Breathing is easier if you have your chest open. You can gesture more easily.

Use your voice

Using your body is one way to own a room. Using your voice is another. Use intonation, volume, and expressiveness to tell your stories and emphasize your points.

If this isn't your natural presentation style, rehearse. You'll feel a bit silly doing it, but projecting your voice will really help you keep the audience's attention.

ALEX ASKS FOR HELP

After venting about the last presentation to her colleague Josh, he offers to help Alex so she can focus more on presenting smoothly. By rehearsing together and looking over the prototype, they catch a couple of mistakes that might have thrown her off before. As a result, she goes into the next presentation much calmer—which comes across to the audience too.

Josh also volunteers to take notes during the meeting, which takes a lot of pressure off Alex since she can now fully focus on questions that come up without having to scramble. With both hands free, Alex is able to use her whole body to bring Norton's story to life by acting it out a bit. This also makes for an engaging and memorable presentation, and the audience respects her time much more as a result. They don't interrupt to ask irrelevant questions, because they're more interested to hear what she has to say next.

Alex has come a long way in improving and refining her presentations. But no presentation is complete without feedback; in fact, that's arguably the most important part. There's an art to giving it and getting it. Let's take a closer look.

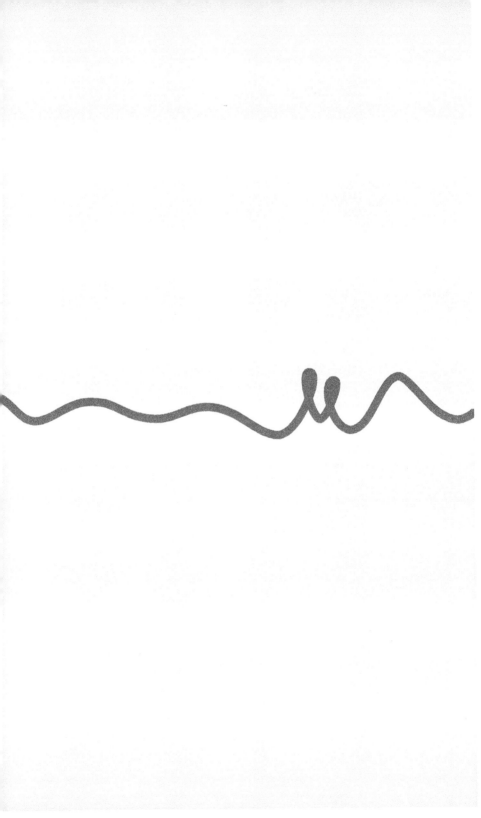

THIS IS THE MOST important chapter of the book! After all, the primary reason for presenting design work is not to show off how amazing you are, but to get input from other people, so you can make the product or service even better.

I'm sure you've been in situations like the one Alex found herself in at the beginning of the book—you've asked for feedback and received a bunch of seemingly random, conflicting comments and opinions that were difficult to address and didn't move the product forward. Or perhaps you just felt that you weren't being heard or were being attacked.

Rethinking how you set up the presentation (covered in Chapters 3 and 4) will put you on the right track. Giving people something specific to address keeps them focused on their expertise, explaining the scope clearly focuses them on what you want feedback on, and showing a person doing a thing focuses on the user, not on the features or screen elements.

The other important aspect, which we'll get into now, is teaching people how to give good feedback.

Good feedback isn't the same thing as praise. Good feedback is feedback you can use to move the product or service forward. It is:

- concrete,
- actionable,
- specific (with examples),
- detailed and clear, and
- based on the person's expertise.

The best way to get this kind of feedback is to teach your stakeholders how to give it. And the best way to do that is with a consistent structure and examples.

A SIMPLE FEEDBACK STRUCTURE

Once you've presented the design, you'll transition to the 'time for questions' that you likely already promised would come at the end. Now that we're here, don't forget that you're still in charge of the presentation. Guide the feedback portion with a few key steps:

- Remind your audience what the scope is (and isn't). "Remember, today we're focusing on how people will get to the product page. We'll go through the product page itself in detail next time."
- Remind them of the jobs you gave them and what they should focus on. "Priya and Grant, do you think this will give local businesses enough exposure that they will be likely to sign up?"

Add some general questions, like these:

- "What are you most looking forward to?" This prompts specifically for positive feedback, which you may not get unless you ask for it.
- "Is there anything that could become a problem?"
- "Was there anything that you expected to see today that I didn't cover?"

Ask people to provide examples to support their comments. "I'm glad to hear you find this more straightforward! Which elements, in particular, do you think are making this a better experience for businesses?"

Note that none of the questions above use the word "like." Never, ever ask ,"What do you think?" or "Do you like it?" You will not get concrete, useful feedback with these questions.

TIMING OF FEEDBACK

You have two options for when to collect feedback—you can either take it at the time of the presentation or get people to give it to you later. There are significant pros and cons to both approaches, so consider how each option might affect the kind of feedback you will get,

Feedback during the presentation

It's great to be able to give a presentation, get feedback while everyone is still present, and collectively discuss and resolve what to do about it. It's collaborative and fast, allowing you to keep the project moving at a good pace. Stakeholders can work together to discuss and make decisions, and have conversations they otherwise wouldn't have. You can literally walk out and start using that feedback in your next phase of work, with clear, agreed-upon direction.

But when I say you will be collecting feedback during the presentation, I mean at the end of your part of the presentation. I strongly suggest you don't take feedback while you're presenting. It breaks the flow of your narrative, and you lose some control of the story. Let people know that you'll take feedback at the end, and they'll usually hold off asking questions while you're presenting. If they do ask a question, let them know that you'll come back to it, and continue the presentation. Do make sure you come back to them, though, or they won't trust that they'll be heard.

You will need to plan a note-taking method and explain to people what they should do before you present your work. An easy method is to ask people to use sticky notes to record their comments. Then at the end, the group puts the sticky notes on a wall, groups them thematically, and discusses them. This is often called affinity diagramming.

Another approach is to have a discussion after the presentation and record the discussion on a whiteboard while you talk about it. This helps people understand that you are listening, that their ideas have been noted, and they can see what decisions the group makes.

Don't ever just have a chat with no visibility about decisions. This makes people feel like you are not listening to them, and they'll be reluctant to contribute later.

Feedback after the presentation

Often there is just not enough time to get feedback on issues in any depth during the presentation. You've shown something to people, asked them to think of issues on the spot, and resolved them quickly. When I've been a stakeholder in this type of situation, I later think about all of the other things that are going to matter and that we didn't get to discuss.

This can be why people often want to discuss things you think you've resolved: You haven't given them the opportunity to reflect properly on what they saw so that they can contribute well. If you don't give people enough time to contribute, they will derail your presentations until their feedback is addressed.

My preference for anything of reasonable complexity is to allow people time to think and provide good feedback. It's slower, but the feedback is infinitely better, more useful, and will lead to a much better product or service.

After the presentation, always send people a message with clear instructions around what you want them to do and how they should do it. Don't rely on people to remember what they've agreed to. Give them a deadline and follow up a few days before the deadline.

Let people give you feedback in a way that is easiest for them, not easiest for you. If you put the burden on them, they either won't do it or will do it poorly. You can offer:

- email,
- a questionnaire,
- a phone call or chat, or
- leaving comments electronically on the prototype.

Then, use whatever organizational system works well for you to track responses. A spreadsheet, document, or database might be all you need. Or you can use bug-tracking or project-tracking software. Just don't lose any feedback.

A potential issue with giving people time to answer is that they will go back to their teams and get feedback from a broader group. This should be a good thing—broader feedback is better for making sure you've uncovered and addressed issues. Do what you can to reach these folks effectively, as covered in Chapter 3, so that their feedback is useful.

FEEDBACK WITHOUT A PRESENTATION

A common approach to showing design work is to send your designs to the client and have them write back to you with questions and feedback. Technology makes this easy; many design tools give you the ability to easily add comments and reply to them within the tool.

This will never be as good as presenting in person (or presenting remotely in person), but it works reasonably well when:

- the design is simple enough that it can be interpreted without a lot of explanation,
- you already have a strong relationship with the client,
- you have taught them how to give good feedback,
- you have taught them how to interpret the designs, and
- you have taught them how to use the software—both for clicking through for a scenario and for leaving comments.

In this case, you'll want to make sure that along with the design files, you send a well-written description covering everything I've suggested you do in person:

- Clarify people's roles and give them particular things to focus on.
- Tell them which parts of the design to focus on and which are out of scope.
- Write out a set of user scenarios that they can follow through themselves.
- Remind them to look at the design at different screen sizes if that's relevant.

Be sure to give them a clear description of when and how to get feedback back to you, too.

ALWAYS ASK FOR FEEDBACK

Should you ever show a design and not ask for feedback? For example, just to show that you have made progress?

I'd suggest not doing that. It's unsatisfying for stakeholders to see work in progress without being able to react to it. It makes them feel like you aren't listening and that they can't contribute. Either make sure you have something to get feedback on or wait until you do.

If you feel like you need to show progress to prove that you are working, consider how you structure your work—why is there nothing you can get feedback on?

MAKING DECISIONS

Whether you collect feedback during the presentation or later, you need to decide what to do with all of it.

My experience is that feedback falls into five categories:

Agree and now

Much of the feedback will be simple changes that the team understands, agrees with, and can be done relatively soon. They go into your to-do list to implement quickly.

Agree and later

Some of the feedback will relate to issues that the team does need to incorporate, but they can't be acted on immediately. These will go into a backlog or added as a feature for later. This category tells people that you are listening and acknowledging that you are going to do something about their requests.

Needs research

Some feedback will be for issues where you don't have enough information to make a decision. They may need some other kind of input, such as:

- additional research with users,
- additional discussion with stakeholders or subject matter experts (beyond clarifications),
- content analysis, or
- analysis of analytics.

Add the research aspect of these into your backlog, and again, let people know that you have listened and will be acting on their feedback.

Clarify

People will often give you feedback that you just don't understand, especially when you take feedback after the presentation. Clarify such feedback quickly and add the clarification into one of the other categories.

No

This is the hardest and most important category.

I think most designers (and product teams) do this particularly poorly, and it can be the main reason stakeholders stop engaging or give the same feedback endlessly.

You must be able to explain why you have decided not to do something about feedback people have given you.

It's relatively easy when they have given you poor-quality feedback: there are usually good reasons why you won't change the color palette or the roundness of the corners on a button.

It's much harder when people have given you high-quality feedback. You have to listen, understand, reflect, and have clear reasons why you aren't going to do something about it. It adds another level of rigor to your decision-making. This is a good thing, but it takes experience and confidence to be able to do it. And it's even harder when you're face-to-face with someone (another advantage of collecting feedback and dealing with it later).

COMMUNICATE IT BACK

After all this good work deciding what feedback you'll act on and what you won't (and why), make sure you communicate this back to stakeholders.

This is the very best way to build up long-term trust. Your audience will know that you've listened to them. They'll learn about what's easy, what's hard, and why. You'll learn more about their actual concerns and constraints.

How you'll do this depends on how your team is set up. You can arrange a meeting to discuss the feedback and issues (particularly around the "no" questions) and collectively make decisions. Once the team is working well together and trusts that you are listening, you can simply email a summary of feedback and decisions. If you store feedback and decisions in a tracking system, you may be able to give everyone access to it.

I suggest you don't address feedback and present new information in the same meeting. Discussing feedback can be difficult. Keep feedback and new work separate. It will also feel like you haven't listened if you are presenting something new before addressing previous issues.

ALEX USES A STRUCTURED FEEDBACK PROCESS

In her last presentation, Alex tried to make some notes and answer questions on the spot.

This time, she plans the feedback process in advance. She takes a few questions in the meeting, answering the simple ones. Josh makes a note of those that need to be followed up on. She lets everyone know she'll send them the slides, so they can go through them in more detail. Then, she asks them to get feedback to her by Friday. Later that day, she emails everyone a follow-up as promised.

When the feedback comes in, she arranges a meeting with the team to go through it and decide what to do about it. They make decisions about changes that are straightforward, and they add some jobs to the backlog for other tasks. One item is out of scope for the project, so they agree not to act on it. Alex prepares a summary of their decisions and sends it to the client, showing them that everything has been considered and letting them know when they can expect to see it incorporated into the designs.

The clients are much happier overall. They know that they contributed and that their contributions were considered, and they're able to understand the reasons behind the project team's decisions, which gives them confidence in the team.

After a few rounds of this presentation and feedback process, the whole team (including the client and stakeholders) are now working very effectively. They are listening to each other and reaching out more to discuss aspects of the design. Questions and comments are very focused, and no one ever asks about a font or the shape of a button. The whole team talks in terms of a person doing a thing.

This is achievable for your projects as well. It may not happen immediately, as you, your team, and your clients may all have to learn a new way of working together. But it will happen faster than you imagined.

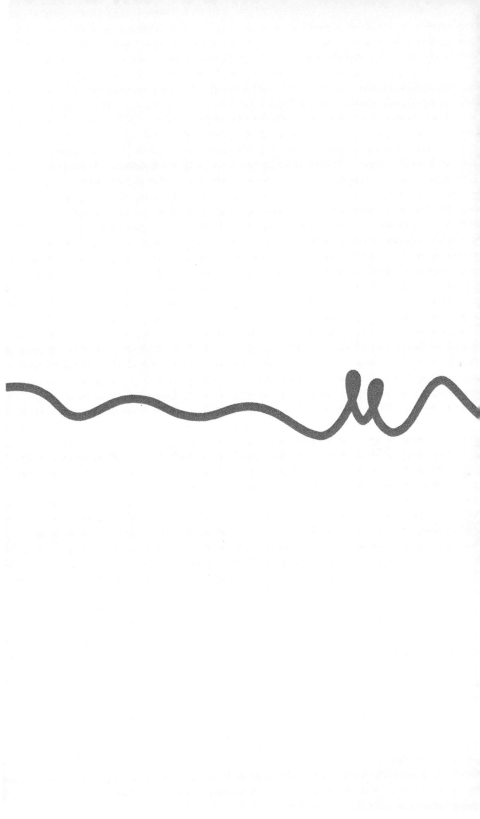

IF I HAD TO summarize my key points in a single presentation slide—well, I wouldn't. I'd make five slides, each containing one strong point:

- Plan for your audience and give everyone a job: They'll contribute their expertise, not their opinion.
- Show the end result, not your progress or process: Your audience will understand what you are showing them and won't get distracted by process details.
- Present a person doing a thing and tell a compelling story: Your audience will give feedback on the story, not the features.
- Set up a clear feedback process and teach your clients how to give great feedback: They will give you relevant and useful feedback.
- Make clear decisions about the feedback and communicate those decisions back to the client: They'll trust that you are listening to them.

With practice, these principles will become second nature. Not only will you feel a lot better about your presentation, but your team will collectively make a much better product.

ACKNOWLEDGMENTS

Naturally, I asked for feedback while writing version 1 of this book (v2 revisions were minor, so I didn't get feedback on this version). I used my own process, told people what I wanted to know about, and gave them clear instructions on how to get it to me. These fine people gave great (not always complimentary, but always useful) feedback and ultimately made the book a lot better: Charlie Lison, Chad Cogdill, Adam Polansky, Sally Bagshaw, Margaret L. Ruwoldt, Matt Fenwick, Josh Line, Justin Thor Hoyer, Claire Agnew, Mags Hanley, Feina You, Natasha Dwyer, Joshua Ogle, and Sarah Stokes. Thank you!

RESOURCES

If you want to dive deeper into presentation skills, or want to learn about how to present other types of work, here are some great books:

- **Banish your Inner Critic, Denise Jacobs**. This is an excellent read that will give you more confidence to stand in front of people, present your ideas, and know your ideas are good.
- **Communicating Design, 2nd ed., Dan Brown**. When I was learning to be a designer, I almost wore out Dan's first edition of this book. The second edition is, of course, just as good. It focuses on the different kinds of diagrams and reports we often present, so it will help a lot if you are still wondering what to present.
- **Communicating the User Experience: A Practical Guide for Creating Useful UX Documentation, Richard Caddick and Steve Cable**. This book is packed full of details about how to create UX deliverables. It's a great read for beginners.
- **Demystifying Public Speaking, Lara Hogan**. Lara provides clear, actionable advice on public speaking—whether you're speaking to a small group or a large group.
- **Design Is a Job** and **You're My Favorite Client, Mike Monteiro**. I group these two books not just because they are by Mike, but because you should read both of them. Together, they will help you work well with clients. It was at a workshop with Mike that I first heard anyone talk about teaching clients how to give feedback, and my presentations became better immediately after.
- **Designing for the Digital Age, Kim Goodwin**. Kim's book covers just about everything you'll need to know to design digital products. It's packed with practical details on the design process, interface design, and so much

more. I mention it here, not only because it is great, but also because it's one of the few books I own that actually covers presenting design work.

- **Discussing Design: Improving Communication and Collaboration through Critique, Adam Connor and Aaron Irizarry**. This book covers how to present to your own team and colleagues. It is the perfect partner and will help you have better design discussions with other designers.

INDEX

ABOUT THE AUTHOR

Donna Spencer is a product designer. She has extensive experience in user experience, service design, workshop facilitation and information architecture. She has worked in government, education, with startups and much more.

She is a regular conference and meetup speaker, article author and has written 5 UX-related books (including this one!). She was the founder of UX Australia and ran it for 9 years. She sews, weaves and knits, and is currently renovating an old house. Her cats are known around the world as they like to 'contribute' to all presentations and meetings.